The Castle That Never Forgets

A. Brailow

BookLeaf Publishing

Presentation by *BookLeaf Publishing*

Web: www.bookleafpub.com

E-mail: info@bookleafpub.com

ISBN: 9789357743600

First edition 2023

To you, whoever and wherever you are.

The Castle That Never Forgets

The castle that never forgets
Feels the scratching of the quills
And the weight of all its debts.

The resident sees silhouettes
Of beauty, of the hope that wills
The castle that never forgets.

The halls' echoes will sing their duets
Of a labyrinthine plot that chills
And the weight of all its debts.

When a conviction shakes and sets,
Beauty opens their bud and stills
The castle that never forgets.

Sudden silence smokescreens deep regrets
That the mirror's vision instills
With the weight of all its debts.

The resident wakes to blurred vignettes
And a single memory that distills
The castle that never forgets
And the weight of all its debts.

Out of Place

Find your "something"
Find a place
Place that feeling
Place a thought
Thoughts are clarity
Thoughts are sudden
Suddenly, thinking makes you feel a little weak
Suddenly, weakness is strength
Strength is hard to find
Strength isn't a priority right now
Now, find solace
Now, find the answer
Answer once, but not coherently
Answer again, but slowly
Again, seek your "something" because your
"something" helps you remember your name
Again, you lift the fog that soaked up your
potential
Potential is more than you realize
Potentially, your potential never stops
Stop your mouth
Stop moving so fast
Fast makes you feel too light
Fast makes everything feel uncomfortable
Uncomfortable is good, you lean into it

Uncomfortable can be too much, you wonder
how to be an asset
Assets keep you grounded
Assets help you escape
Escape, just for now
Escape your story
Stories aren't static
Stories can be rewritten
Rewrite one word
Rewrite one line
Line everything up until it looks neat
Lines don't always look like that
That helps because looking put together was
always too much of a focus for you
That helps you realize that you don't need to be
perfect
Perfect, they say, doesn't exist
Perfect is something that cannot be fixed
Fixed is not what we want to be
Fixed, still, is the gaze
Gaze, again, means discomfort
Gaze and, then, turn the page
Page through, first and then
Page again and again
Again, find your "something" before
"something" gives out
Again, there's "something" that's been left out
Out of the forest
Out, away from the path

Path
Forest

Always

"Why" is elusive
and "Why" changes shape.
"Why" became a monster that day.
"Why" buzzed and flew and whispered in my
ears.
"Why" hid under tables and, then, disappeared.

As soon as I decided my search was over,
"Why" decided to perch on my shoulder.
"Why" was heavy and sharp, and it didn't make
sense.
"Why" was a secret that never stood a chance.

As soon as "Why" needed to make an
appearance,
"Why" decided to break into less than
coherence.
For that, I had to take the blame
Even though "Why" kept practically screaming
my name.

"Who" took a backseat,
"How" and "Where" were blasé.
"What" wasn't an option.
"When" was a pain.

Not too late, I discovered I
Wasn't even the one who needed "Why".

"Why" can be important.
"Why" can be a friend.
"Why" can be the anchor from the start to the
end.

All I want to know is, "Will I be okay?"
And if the answer is, "Always."

Aversion

The rainwater was reminded to fall from the
clouds,
 and so it fell, but not straight down.
 The water rode the wind that curved and drove
 some of the droplets to a roof,
 some to a river,
 some to a sidewalk,
 some to a road,
 some to the storm drain,
 some to a bird bath,
 some to buckets,
 some to flowerpots,
 and many to places where it kept rushing
 and running
 and slipping.
 Because the rainwater was reminded to fall
from the clouds,
 it did not fall straight down.

 The leaf was reminded to fall from the tree
 when Autumn's breath turned it a soft orange
and red,
 and so it fell, but not straight down.
 The leaf joined its family that rode the wind that
curved and drove

some of the leaves into pieces,
some to a lawn,
some to windows,
some to the ground,
some to windshields,
some to upturned faces,
some to lost things,
some to the bottoms of shoes,
and many to piles of leaves from other trees
where they stayed
flat
and still.
Because the leaf was reminded to fall from the
tree,
when Autumn's breath turned it a soft orange
and red,
it did not fall straight down.

A creative mind was reminded that their
inclinations weren't of value,
and so it fell, but not straight down.
The mind clutched its passion and clung to its
enthusiasm that curved and drove
it into its parts and pieces,
some from memories,
some from sentiment,
some from resourcefulness,
some from adaptability,
some from the ability to think beyond,

some from its intended structure,
and many from their questions which turned to
aversion
from what would have built
a better world.
Because a creative mind was reminded that
their inclinations weren't of value,
it fell,
but it did not fall straight down.

Name the Universe

If I understand her,
I know the way she looks
When she doesn't remember the words,
but she's happy to be where she is.

If I understand her,
I know the way she speaks
When the week has been long,
and a compassionate warmth passes between us.

If I understand her,
I know the way she pauses
When we get to where we're going,
and she hides one eye with her hair.

If I understand her,
As I understand more
About each moment
About each word
About each expression
Learn every exception
And ask each time
Just in case,
I will know enough to,
As someone once said,
"Name the universe."

Resilience

The bowl was crudely made.
 Crude, with jagged edges
 that felt rough against my hands.
 Crude, but I held it
 as if it were as smooth as the floor I stood on.

 The bowl was crudely made.
 As I carried it across the room,
 words of praise echoed in my ears.
 Confident.
 Steady.
 Resilient, as my feet traced infinity on the
smooth floor.

 The bowl was crudely made.
 Crude, with jagged edges
 that began to dig into my skin
 as eyes gazed forward,
 and I carried it across the room
 while words of praise echoed in my ears.

 Confident.
 Steady.
 Resilient.

The bowl was crudely made.
Crude, and when I reached the line at the end of
the room,
drawn on the smooth floor,
I stopped.
The words silenced.
The bowl was crudely made,
and could not be removed
from my hands.

What I've Never Heard

Tell me what I've never heard.
Hear me whisper like a bird.
Birds gather in the bushes there,
but for what's above them,
they do not care.

Tell me now, because you care,
caring is what you would dare.
Dare to step within my bounds,
until whispers of birds
no longer sound.

Some were the days I did not sleep.
These were the days I heard no peace.
Birds gathered closely near my door,
but what was near,
they would ignore.

Tell me what I've never heard.
Tell me now, because you care,
that some were the days I did not sleep.

Unravel

On the day I unravel,
 I must not be seen,
 except by the ancient trees.

I, placed within the movement of this wind,
Placed with meaning,
Placed with intent,
Placed in buildings with no doors,
Placed under high arches
Placed next to yours.

On the day I unravel,
I must not be seen,
except by the wind that moves me.

I, placed in the hollow of an ancient tree,
Placed in silence,
Placed easily,
Placed where hope endures,
Placed and posed,
Placed next to yours.

On the day I unravel,
I must not be seen,
except by the ancient trees.

Vertigo

Danger loves tall buildings,
 so we held each other back from the edge
 that made an unseen force press
 on our heads
 and throats.

We held each other back from the edge,
 just like we said we would,
 until the clouds rained
 on the river,
 and an unseen force rushed
 to our eyes
 and to our fingertips.

Just like we said we would,
 we held each other back from the edge,
 but not to break
 from the danger that loves tall buildings.

We held each other back from the edge,
 to make room
 for the unseen force that moved
 from our feet
 to our knees
 to our arms.

The Gate

They forgot what never would
and only saw what could
and might.

They forgot what always is
and only saw what may
and past.

Then, when faced with what always was,
they tried to catch what could
and might.

Finding nothing, there they stood,
at the gate, dented, dull,
and cracked.

Peering into what always was,
the lens was blurred,
they had to be led.

Beyond the gate of "never would",
all that could not be found had stood,
but all that could not be found had waited
patiently, not knowing why
what never would
was so close by.

Heartbeat

On top of the beat,
 there was still
 peace, yet agitation.
 By agitation, I mean,
 movement.
 I mean,
 that moment when your nose wrinkles,
 but only from dust.

It was powerful.
 There was still
 peace, yet a stirring. By a stirring, I mean,
 movement.
 I mean,
 what you do in your sleep when dreams move
you,
 but only from worlds,
 from a mind unfurled.

On top of the beat,
 there was still
 peace, yet I feel.
 I feel, I mean,
 I feel something.
 At least, that's what I call it.

I mean,
as my voice broke,
it was not because it was thrown.
It was caught
by an echo.

Words

If I had to put words to it, I would say,
 our voices overlapped.
It was when we
heard the drums.

If I had to put words to it, I would say,
the drums spoke our intentions.
It was when we
shared sight.

If I had to put words to it, I would say,
our eyes met, but not in a way I recognized.
It was when we
shared the same thought.

If I had to put words to it, I would say,
we knew we'd be home in a minute.
It was when we
built a bridge of arms,
and arms that fell.

If I had to put words to it, I would say,
the guards rested, as we gave them leave.
It was when
the roads were long and winding,

but your door was close.
It was when
the water rushed,
but the candle burned.

If I Could Build

If I could build,
 I'd build a dove.
 A dove that flies
 over swamps
 and trees.

If I could build,
 I'd build a tree,
 unhollowed, green,
 shading,
 and free.

If I could build,
 I'd build a ground
 with bumps and cracks,
 moved
 by the wind.

If I could build
 as I cannot,
 I'd build what lives.
 Peace.
 Protection.
 Purpose.

The Light

They became the tide.
They became the force of
what can never be,
never knowing
it is.

They became the tide,
swirling around my arms,
holding them up,
throwing me against the sand,
and again.

They became the tide,
that punished as long as
the tide never became me.
The tide never became
a state that is not water,
a state that does not push or pull,
a state that is not in stasis,
or a state that is in constant flow,
when you thought "flow" was for water,
and what it was meant to do.

They became the tide
that tried to erode,

but I became the light.

They became the tide,
resentful of the light,
that they could only hope
for its reflection.

Nothing

Nothing came into my room.
 The air was thick with
nothing, which rode on its current
around my head,
whispering in my ears
that nothing
was in my room.

Nothing stayed as I left.
Even in my rush, forward
and forward,
beside my shoulder,
whispering in my ears
that nothing
was in my room.

Nothing chose to follow me.
The static in its wake was caused by
nothing, on all sides
as wheels rolled under my feet
in a way I did not see
as the air was thick with
nothing, which rode on its current
outside my window,
whispering in my ears

that nothing
would follow me outside the doors
and down the block
and right.

Nothing sat next to me.
When I showed my ticket,
and empty spaces turned to eyes,
blinded briefly by the voice of home
before closing,
burned.

Once

Once upon a time, the stars
 wished, this time, to heal what's barred.
 Tucked beside the flower's stem
 was the seed of what would begin.
 The lady said that she must sell.
 The stars did not have more to tell.

Once upon a wish, the seed
 was brought to a house near a willow tree.
 The lady begged and hushed its sound
 only she could hear, so no solace was found.
 The beetles clung to the basket's edge.
 The lady waved them away to the window
ledge.
 The frogs surrounded her at her feet.
 She called to the swallow in summer's heat.

Once upon a summer's day,
 inside a satchel, the dormant seed would stay.
 At least for now, as the lady moved,
 and the swallow's perch on her shoulder
resumed.

The lady said to the swallow, new to flight,

"May you never remember me this day or this night,
 but befriend my likeness if you please.
 She will not walk the world with ease.
 This world was not built with her needs in mind,
 but as her friend, show her that some are kind.
 Give her the space she needs to grow,
 but remind her she never need be alone."

Once upon clumsy departing wings,
 the lady heard the swallow sing.
 She then softly knocked on the house's door
 in a story that was told before.
 A kind woman answered, and as you recall,
 The lady said, "Is there nothing you wish for at all?"
 The seed rattled and glowed, knowing this was the time,
 and into her story she would climb.

Poison

They spoke, and poison filled their cup.
The fumes lightly touched my nose.
They expected eyes on the visible steam
working its way to the window
to the world.

Yet.

When eyes looked directly into their own,
it was a consequence they'd never known.
To drink the poison again.
To drink it again, and to speak the words,
and fill their cup
until their body becomes its vessel
while eyes looked directly into their own.
It was a circle they'd never known.

If only to scream.
If only to fluster.
If only to bring forth words that would
humor the poison and add to its flame.

They spoke, the poison overflowing,
yearning for what would sweeten its taste.
That's what everybody said would happen.

The silence was such a profound presence
accompanying the shaking hand
that drew the poison
to their lips again.

The Promise

From the moment you began your ABC's,
Learning history, science, and 1-2-3's,
A question you might hear or see
is of what you truly want to be.

No matter what you might enjoy
Writing, math, art, or building toys
There's something for everyone
and time to decide.
Maybe you know what you want to be.

You might be a teacher, an astronaut,
An artist, a doctor, but no matter what,
You'll find amazing ways to change people's
lives,
and encourage them all to always be kind.

Whoever you are or choose to be,
up in the air, on the ground, on the seas.
Whether you know what you want
Or you're still deep in thought,
You are free to be yourself with me.

Whether you need to try again,
Whether you need a helping hand,

Whoever who you are or choose to be,
You are free to be yourself with me.

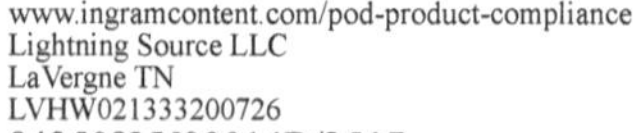